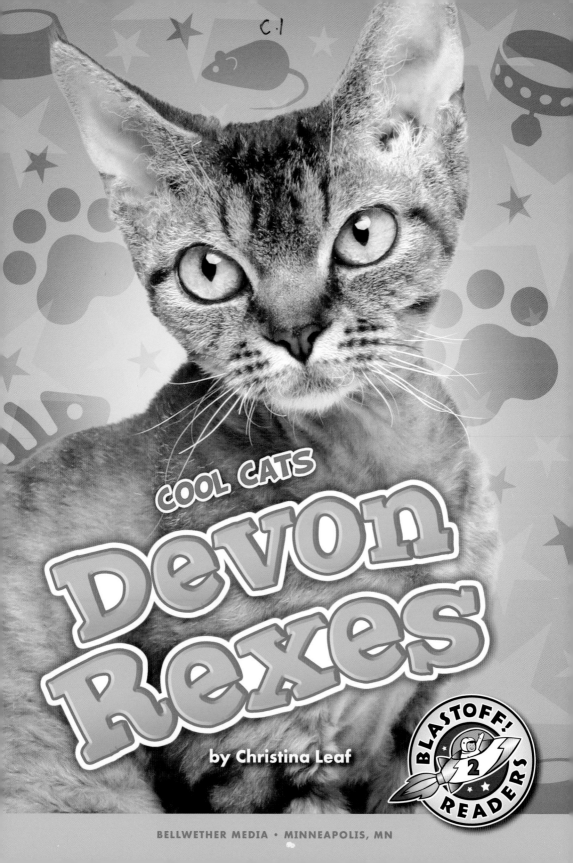

C.1

COOL CATS

Devon Rexes

by Christina Leaf

BLASTOFF! READERS 2

BELLWETHER MEDIA • MINNEAPOLIS, MN

Note to Librarians, Teachers, and Parents:

Blastoff! Readers are carefully developed by literacy experts and combine standards-based content with developmentally appropriate text.

Level 1 provides the most support through repetition of high-frequency words, light text, predictable sentence patterns, and strong visual support.

Level 2 offers early readers a bit more challenge through varied simple sentences, increased text load, and less repetition of high-frequency words.

Level 3 advances early-fluent readers toward fluency through increased text and concept load, less reliance on visuals, longer sentences, and more literary language.

Level 4 builds reading stamina by providing more text per page, increased use of punctuation, greater variation in sentence patterns, and increasingly challenging vocabulary.

Level 5 encourages children to move from "learning to read" to "reading to learn" by providing even more text, varied writing styles, and less familiar topics.

Whichever book is right for your reader, Blastoff! Readers are the perfect books to build confidence and encourage a love of reading that will last a lifetime!

This edition first published in 2016 by Bellwether Media, Inc.

No part of this publication may be reproduced in whole or in part without written permission of the publisher. For information regarding permission, write to Bellwether Media, Inc., Attention: Permissions Department, 5357 Penn Avenue South, Minneapolis, MN 55419.

Library of Congress Cataloging-in-Publication Data

Leaf, Christina.
  Devon Rexes / by Christina Leaf.
      pages cm. – (Blastoff! Readers. Cool Cats)
  Summary: "Relevant images match informative text in this introduction to Devon rexes. Intended for students in kindergarten through third grade"– Provided by publisher.
  Audience: Ages 5-8.
  Audience: K to grade 3.
  Includes bibliographical references and index.
  ISBN 978-1-62617-309-5 (hardcover : alk. paper)
  1. Rex cat–Juvenile literature. I. Title.
  SF449.R4L43 2016
  636.8'22–dc23
                      2015028719

Table of Contents

What Are Devon Rexes?   4

History of Devon Rexes   8

Elfish Looks   12

Playful Pixies   16

Glossary   22

To Learn More   23

Index   24

What Are Devon Rexes?

Devon rexes are cats with curly hair. Their short, wavy **coats** are famous around the world!

Their short whiskers also curl.

Devon rex cats are called
Devons for short.

The *rex* in their name comes from the cats' fur. It is soft like the fur of rex rabbits.

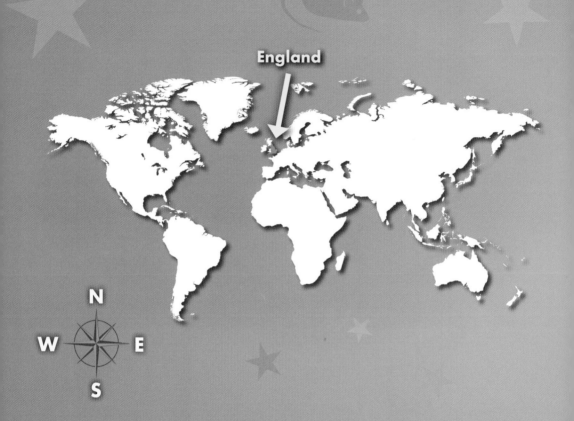

England

N
W • E
S

In 1960, a woman named Beryl Cox found an unusual kitten in Devon, England.

The kitten had a curly coat!
Miss Cox named him Kirlee
for his fur.

Miss Cox **bred** Kirlee with other cats. In time, more curly-coated kittens were born.

Kirlee was the first of a
new **breed**!

Elfish Looks

Devons are covered in waves or soft curls. They may be one color or patterned.

Devon Rex Coats

point

calico

tabby

solid

Some Devons have **point coats**.
Other coats are **calico** or **tabby**.

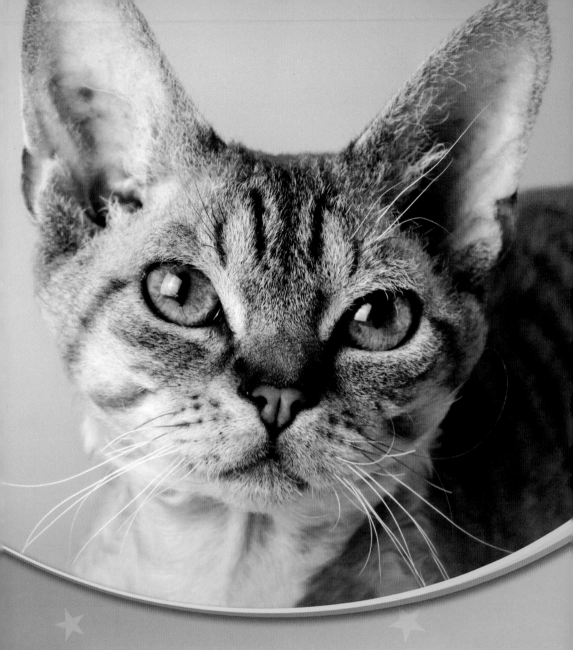

Devons have **slender** bodies and necks. Huge ears give the cats elfish looks. Their large eyes come in many colors.

Devon Rex Profile

— big ears

— large eyes

— long, skinny neck

— short, curly coat

Weight: 6 to 9 pounds (3 to 4 kilograms)

Life Span: 9 to 15 years

Playful Pixies

The cats are **affectionate**. They like to be held and snuggle under blankets.

Devons also get along with other pets.

Devon rexes are active and playful. They explore everything high and low.

These **curious** cats
can jump well.

Some people call Devons
pixies. They are **mischievous**
and often cause trouble.

They are always hungry. Some will steal food from their owners' plates!

21

Glossary

affectionate—loving

bred—purposely mated two cats to make kittens with certain qualities

breed—a type of cat

calico—a pattern that has patches of white, black, and reddish brown fur

coats—the hair or fur covering some animals

curious—interested or excited to learn or know about something

mischievous—having a playful desire to cause trouble

pixies—small fairies that like to cause trouble

point coats—light-colored coats with darker fur in certain areas; pointed cats have dark faces, ears, legs, and tails.

slender—thin

tabby—a pattern that has stripes, patches, or swirls of colors

To Learn More

AT THE LIBRARY

Finne, Stephanie. *Devon Rex Cats*. Minneapolis, Minn.: ABDO Publishing, 2015.

Hengel, Katherine. *Delightful Devon Rexes*. Edina, Minn.: ABDO, 2012.

Sexton, Colleen. *The Life Cycle of a Cat*. Minneapolis, Minn.: Bellwether Media, 2011.

ON THE WEB

Learning more about Devon rexes is as easy as 1, 2, 3.

1. Go to www.factsurfer.com.

2. Enter "Devon rexes" into the search box.

3. Click the "Surf" button and you will see a list of related web sites.

With factsurfer.com, finding more information is just a click away.

Index

bodies, 14
bred, 10
breed, 11
coats, 4, 9, 10, 13, 15
colors, 12, 13
Cox, Beryl, 8, 9, 10
curly, 4, 5, 9, 10, 12, 15
Devon, England, 8
ears, 14, 15
explore, 18
eyes, 14, 15
fur, 7, 9
jump, 19
Kirlee, 9, 10, 11
kitten, 8, 9, 10
life span, 15
name, 6, 7
necks, 14, 15
owners, 21

patterns, 12, 13
pets, 17
pixies, 20
rabbits, 7
size, 15
snuggle, 16
steal, 21
trouble, 20
wavy, 4, 12
whiskers, 5

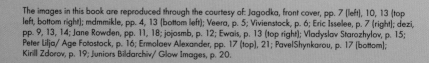